janet gray

Illuminati

Poems in the book also appeared in the following publications:

Amelia, Cat's Eye, Corners, Exquisite Corpse, Gypsy, Hanging Loose, Impetus, Nude Erections, Open 24 Hours, Orpheus, Orphic Lute, Pasadena Weekly, "Poetry Loves Poetry" (Momentum Press), *Planet Detroit, Sierra Madre Review, Tandava, To Pull Out The Peachboy* (Illuminati) and *Truly Fine*

Illuminati

P.O. Box 67E07 Los Angeles 90067

Made In U.S.A.

ISBN: 0-89807-136-4

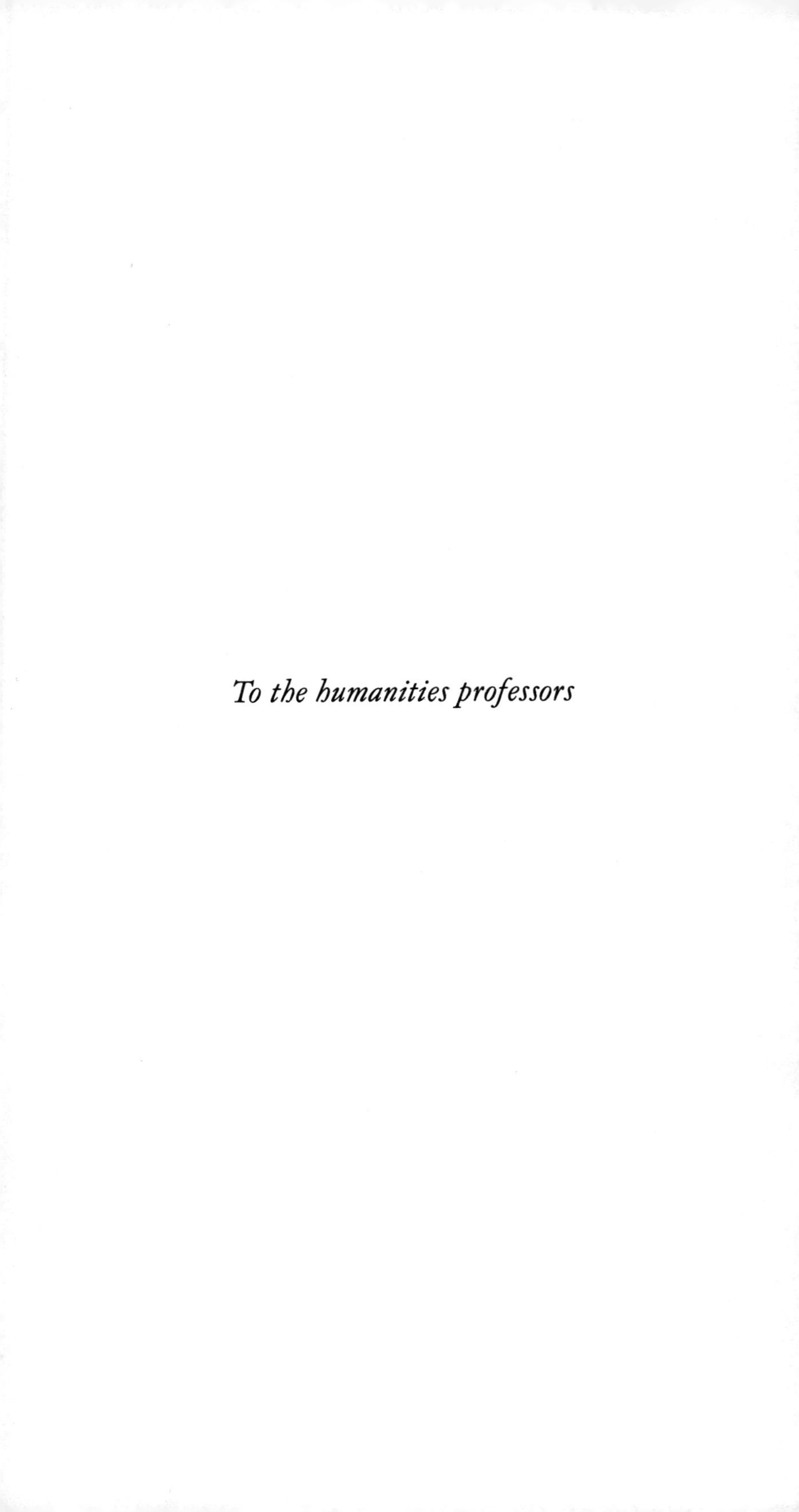

To the humanities professors

· *DO NOT TRY TO PULL UP ANYTHING BY THE ROOT* ·

Do not try to pull up anything by the root
when it is rooted in soft material.

Do not try to pull out the peachboy,
even gently with tweezers.

Things that are watery and thin-skinned
seem to grow all by themselves,
but they are barely alive.

Once I unravelled myself entirely
thinking I had to take gifts sensibly
and at the right time.

You can't see the little faces
under the top of the soil,
but they are there.

· *THE POINT OF A STRANGE MAN* ·

The point of a strange man is
to get released to his custody.
Let him see you in the window.
He looks vague against the light,
and wants something unspeakable.

EXTRICATION ·

Carry your drill across the yard
in such a way that they cannot
bring any charges against you.

They'll be mad. They'll know you've gone
too far. You are going to drill a hole
in the cell wall,

the way the strange man drilled into you —
left you overripe and pushing
overripe fruit into little holes in the wall.

· *OF FALSE DELIGHT* ·

If you walked into my bathroom
and reached for me in the water
you would be mine you would be my
    sweet boy

what you would be worth to me
is joy
      the dozens of watertoys
stacked beside the tub

I would twist apart and float on the water
look! look at the floating
armless men and women and the lurching water!

· *I Have A Passion For Men Who Need Women Imprisoned In Timelessness* ·

I have a passion for men who need women
    imprisoned in timelessness:
that I should talk to them until I lose words,
that I should please them until I lose pleasure,
that I should listen to their music until I
    have none of my own

I have none of my own:
there is only the deep beating
drum, and the passion for children
    who have no fathers

· *IF I COULD WEAR THE PAIN* ·

If I could wear the pain
like perfume, for example —
a habit, a way of telling
who I am;

       if the source of it
could become unimportant,
or simply interesting — the stories I tell
in a candid voice —

about orphans, meeting them, unwillingly
leading a pack of them down the street;
to be — not steely, but also not
in search of compassion —

sad, instead of eager
and uncertain about how I should act
if, for example, I mistake a strange man
for my father;

       if it could all become
the soft lines that crease and fade
in lovemaking —
but never entirely fade —

· *THE FLOWERMAKER* ·

Your daughter is not dead, but sleeping.

Feel how the heart is a flower, frozen
mid-bloom.
The pain is because a flower should open.
There was a war, all the music was full of guns,
everything shattered
and fell away. You were orphans
and you made your child an orphan.
The stone of a fruit after the flesh
has fallen off.
She was born with numb hands.

I worked with my hands —
twisted flowers from swatches of silk,
knotted floss to the hem of a white sheet.
But my hands stopped working.

There's nothing I can do for the child.
Sometimes I write my name on her
with my finger —
it's like a stick scratching dust.
But remember how you bent to catch her
when she came glistening out of you.

· WHAT I CANNOT REMAKE BY DIVING ·

What I cannot remake by diving
into deep water
into the belly of a fish
I will remake with months of labor
in the land of the dead

cutting, and carving,
and shaving, and bleaching,
and I will use those parts as if they felt.

· *IF YOU PLUCK A ROSE APART* ·

If you pluck a rose apart —
carefully! —
and arrange the parts in rows
by size and color —
what you have is:
the parts of a dead rose;

and there are those
who will be grateful
that, at last,
the heart is exposed.

· *1956* ·

The wind has arms
and that I know.
He must have a mouth
or how can he blow?
The wind has eyes
with which he spies
me walking by,
either wet or dry.
The wind has wings
or how could he fly
through the sky
and pass me by?

· *I Could Break You* ·

I could break you,
I could swing up my false leg and break you

(it will be like building a campfire in the
    wilderness,
all alone: late at night,
picking at the parts of you and piling them
you will become one spot of glow on
    the black land
and I a single shadow inside you
holding myself with a blanket around me
rocking a little and gazing with love,
    with love)

· *MOUNT RAINIER* ·

If you leave me I will stay where I am
pitched against a stump that rots with the thaw
and if you come back you will not find me
and if you speak I won't answer.

I'll shove my hands in my womb and not blink
and I will just stay cold in the snow.
Everyone will think I died of exposure.

· *THE EIGHTIES* ·

These are the years when at last I will know
what is so urgent — a message to you,
    or some other man.

I want to tell you about my fear of war.

I will come to you in a dark overcoat,
my hair wet and tangled,
crazed in a way you can't imagine.

"Martin!" I'll say, grasping your wrists.
"Don't waste any time!" Then I'll vanish.

· *I'VE SPENT THE DAY ALONE* ·

I've spent the day alone
along the waters of the estuary.
What is an estuary?
No, that's not it.

The truth is I'm waiting
for everyone to come home.
Haven't been blessed
like this for so long.

Alone with the old wood,
the deep rich colors,
and time, light and rain
and my own private follies.

Here is a list
of types of flowers:
neutral, fine, and disparate;
stable and accurate —

fossil-like and lizard-tail-like
(in that it detaches
from the Living Creature
when roughly handled.)

· *People Who Like Me Quiet* ·

People who like me quiet
leave when I open my mouth.
People who like me when I talk
don't know when I'm lying.

I get hungry and think
about eating the people. I want
them to wait while I take a nap
and then I want them to leave.

Dear Professor McGann, pardon this
intrusion if that's what it is; but
today is my first day in this house.
At about 3:30, most of the
humanities professors — the greyheads —
came to my kitchen and helped themselves
to coffee. They ate up my pecan swirls.
They leaned on the furniture talking about
civilization. Was this house once
the humanities faculty lounge? That
would be understandable, since my
back door is just across a green patch from
the back door of the humanities building. I
know it's hard to change a habit. But
they didn't seem to realize I live here. They
ignored me — no, they did ask for cremora.
I was washing up the mugs when I
saw you through the window. You were
on the back steps of the humanities
building staring into space. Don't you
like these conversations? I quickly
put my shoes on, but then
decided not to bother you. Thus,
this note. Did *you* know I was here?

1.

At first I gag on both of them. More violently on
father than on mother. Father's flesh is leathery
and resists; the point is to destroy, not eat. With
mother, a hunt for food, but rage prevents it—
and loathing. This is dead flesh, out of tune.
Hungrier and hungrier. I chew until it's mush—
then it slides down. I didn't mean to swallow! But
now I've done it and that's that. But I don't have
to digest.

2.

I want to take you apart
No more fingers, no more muscular arms
    wrapped in fat and bad skin
No more toes that crack
No death
No more parents that come to an end

3.

There is a place I go on these long afternoons.
   There
where the air in the afternoon is sweet
and green, I go about conceiving. Oh,

no, it is not a fish or a newt this time.
You are not invited yet. But one day
you might come, maroon and jarring.

· *HILL STATION* ·

how green
everything is and the air
clean   what does it matter
I'm right on the edge
of the stream and normal
only since yesterday   house
clean again and aired out
tea roses blooming

I don't mind your mentioning
his name
slice him with bamboo leaves
cover him with horse leeches
let's go up the stream

· *IN PREPARATION* ·

Some come slowly
and are hard work.
You see it rolling up
through the trees:
a fog. In a minute,
it will hold you.

In this other part
of the forest,
where the most savage
flowers bloom —
you never thought
you'd find this place
again —
          sing,
because you want
to live forever.

· *TYPING* *·*

There is the thought of summer
homelessness
parents far away
summer in mountains where the green is
    musclebound
and though the body is still bound
to the chair at night, and
the gut is cut with coffee,
There is the articulate intelligence of tiny bones
nesting in bright ivy
a long march a distant war in black uniforms
exile in black uniforms
the fingers flap faster than sight
the mind hovers hums dives
I have made few mistakes, but I have
    made some
and there is no excuse,
they must all be corrected

· *MAMMA'S LEFT BREAST* ·

if i had a chance
to repair your chest mamma
i would   put back that
blob of fat & associated
musculature straighter than prosthesis &
sane again   some macho asshole recently
told me "our children are our
assassins"   i nodded because i
know   tried it with you
not in my fantasies did
your precious cells get
gynecidal blight though yes i
did wish myself into a
different world from yours
fucked all night in a
basement in the barrio
mamma   but how could you
let that take off your
breast   not even the right one
to be an amazon   if
i were stronger than you
i would have children

· THINGS THAT PULL APART IN SORTING ·

a summer night in a southern city,
some years ago, and: my father's anger.

the one: children who have seen moon
landings before, and know how it is done;

and the other: a quick slice below the belt,
his good mouth still not fouled.

I am making the things fall into separate piles:

litter where the air is too thin,
and judgment;

a scarred breast,
the sweet faraway voice of a man;

and at last, a child is calling,
over a long distance, but she can be heard —

how sad that we were all fooled!
I am the worker, in men's white working clothes.

· *AFTER RICH* ·

Thirteen years ago came back to "LA."
    The treelined streets
almost the same. A new second story here,
    new paint there,
a fence tight against a front door.
Collapsing garden. Top of Kenneth Way
    amputated,
where our house was still vestigial nerves.

The white bitch I ran with at dusk
on the edge of the Arroyo Seco: dead
since nineteen seventy. She was an example
to me: stumplegged
mix of German hound and English terrier
    (spayed)
flying the distance between blackening oaks.

· *I Spent My Infancy In A Used Clothing Warehouse* ·

balanced on bales of American castoffs
smelling burlap and thick ink

my father baled the clothes, wired
the bags closed, stenciled them FOR EUROPE

and stenciled the sharp black and red
eight-point Quaker star

borrowed from French ambulances in the
First World War

he moved fast, made noise with a machine
I admired our power
as a team

to engulf a chaos of colors in scratchy sacks
and boldly sign them

and I grew up in the things too frivolous
or soiled for Europe

· *FOR BOBBI* ·

I write facing a window at night
& you I am writing to, you are not out there.
An oak tree. A scraggly lawn out there
somewhere in the dark. My room. My face
dim & quizzical on the glass. But you are
    nowhere.

For a long time I knew
there was no point in magnifying the face.
I objected to the vulgarity of the face.
The mirror & trimmings around the dressing
    table.
The lighting all wrong & no point in light.

Still I look at my face in every piece of
    glass, I look for you
big sister, & here in front of the night window
is where I put myself in a trance
& die a little, debase myself for you.

· *PUBLIC LIFE* ·

Day after day I go to City Hall
to complain about acts of God
such as the huge eucalyptus bough
that fell on my genitalia.

The distant trumpeting of my body
wakes me at dawn. My bare feet
slap the pavement. The angel at the gate
admits them, one at a time.

I stand before the officials,
desolate. They are threatened
by my awful smell. My armpits
are a rupture in civilization.

Secretly, I hoard lies. I've lied
to boards of directors.
I've lied about my taste in food.
My passion — strange flowers that go to seed —
blooms in the courtyard of City Hall.

If only City Hall were a huge mother!
I'd crawl into her lap, convulsed in shame.

· *Dreammusic Made Safe* ·

The percussion section takes its instruments up to the second balcony and drops them.

A selected area of the orchestra has been cordoned off and labeled perhaps "Reserved."

First balcony seats are most coveted.

Funds for the repair and/or replacement of the upholstery were generously granted by the Mildred and Marion Michener Foundation for Music and Social Change. (Thanks to Bandolero Upholsterers.)

Areas adjacent to the "Reserved" section are labeled "Hard Hat Required."

To raise funds to repair and/or replace the percussion section, hard hats engraved with the symphony's logo are sold in the lobby for a sliding scale suggested donation (tax deductible). (Gratitude to Teamster's Local 457 Cultural Foundation for matching funds.)

The extra fancy people and the people with supposed ceremonial relationships to this performance and the parties therein, whom the audience will expect to see ushered to the Reserved section, will not appear.

The percussion section retrieves its instruments.

· *THE SYNTHESIZER* ·

For this, my sweet,
you murdered our sixth major
credit account: sirens; jets crashing
on a rocky shore;
neurotic laughter of the
Mormon Tabernacle Choir; secret sound
of green cheese curing in
the middle of the moon.

I am so mean
but you & your instrument are
obscene, robbing the celesta, raping
the harpsichord of her chink.
Makes me happy —
houseful of unnatural noise &
no strings, no heavy metal,
nothing but disturbed air.

Go on, Home Federal,
hover around the squashed pride
of our prostitutes' hearts. Urgent calls
& our names on neat
labels daily denounce the outrage
of our account's red throat. Between
jobs we play & the dust
of our credit sings.

things flow through
the strainer   pale
brown flowers are left
behind   after the tablecloth
is stained and the fingers
strained from pressing
against each other   after
the tablecloth comes off
stained it will never
never come clean   I will not
tell you I am not
a simple girl   I
am not a white bird
flying over cities and
forgetting them
after the tablecloth
is stained everyone
leaves the room
the door shuts   the
prisms tremble   after
the lights dim
the colors all land
on each other   old friends
examine each other's hands
and find they are both older
after the crystal
is abandoned   the lights
turned down   nothing
is happening out in
the rain   after
the white birds all tuck

their heads under their wings
after the tablecloth is
stained there is no
reason to start the ignition

There is a passion in the movement of air
I am sending you a passion through the
    regular and repeating movement of air

Learned what I know from the boys down
    the street at the jr. high
& the girls on stage lipsynching the great
    popular passions
every day in fall
when first they come back they make this
    over the air

i am not practiced

i am the messenger.
you across the street
once i knew
that in the back you had a paradise of
    gleopholosis & shade
sunspattered jackhorn trees
you are the ones holding the mystery of
    bolt blast wicked keep & hold & keep
    tight keep secret.

first light
crossing the machine
bullseye on the retina under the eyelids the
    flow of blood the spots of penetrating light

Where the borders are open
friends travel with no assignment

They are interesting for where they sleep
in spite of their fake money

They don't wallow in your dreams
or lurk in the drapes

You have mornings of true solitude
fists around the breasts

Each friend has a particular ache
and acts like a stranger

They meet you at a mirror
as if you were royalty

You don't scold them for being crude
when the light is draining

They lie beside you
all beauty and sense

And nothing softens you
like being taken out finally at night

· *ETYMOLOGY OF "OOBLECK"* ·

(Dr. Seuss: *Bartholomew and the Oobleck*)

oocyte   female gametocyte
oozy
oomph
oology   eggs
oolong   black dragon
oo = eggs
oosphere
oosperm
cockroach egg case
  ootheca
  ooze
bleck - black grease
     - to write
     - to blacken

· _YEAR AFTER YEAR THE SAME THINGS COME DOWN FROM MY SKY_ ·

Certain areas of the sea of Japan
are sensitive, like skin
and if you hover or pass over
them, you will come down.

You might be a hot fog full of eggs
or the ooze of a dragon.
You might be a white man
packed in a case.

Whatever pot you were cooked up in,
you run on my black grease
and break out your messages
in my air space.

I can't stand you in my air.
I cannot bear your noise
or your hardware
or your sticky eyes.

You cannot understand
this mystic hole,
this sensitive black growth
in a white shell.

And if you dare
invade my skin
I will come up and get you
and take you down.

· THE DROWNING — HIROSHIMA 1955 ·

Maidens on the banks of the river
mocking the lumpy scars on each other's thighs:
Yours is a frog an evil one with huge warts.
Oh yeah well yours,
yours is the fat man smoking his pipe
and the smoke goes all the way up there.
That was going too far.

Here comes the perfect maiden
the one without scars.
Where were you when the bomb dropped,
inside a pumpkin?
Where were you when the fire came
and the shelters collapsed,
under the fat man?
No one deserves to be a daughter
of the wrecked city if her thighs are clean:
no elephant headstands, no cracked bark,
no broken sailing ships in the pattern of
    her skin.

When you swim in the river,
sister flatskin, we dare you
swim out as far as you can.
When you start to drown, we'll save you.

· *ANY REPLACEMENT FOR GOD MUST BE FUNNY* ·

If you were now to start, old Apollonian,
your sermon to the young boys standing guard,
you could not start with the idea of the sun.

You must give up the idea of the idea.
The inconceivable blew up two towns
before you died, before the boys were born.

And we have seen the image of the thing
more elegant and powerful than god
in the privacy of our apartments.

That picture on the box is not our fiction.
It was the fact about molecular revolt
seen clearly in its idea by men of reason.

How pure the vast ascension of the bits
of mind and concrete, Pontiac and chicken
that expels us and our images . . .

And yet how like a criminal visitation
from the fire horses and their bright god
bent on savaging the earth's green women.

This, of course, is nonsense. But that the sun
has tens of thousands of unhatched relatives
is fact, is not idea or abstraction.

And since those towns blew up, the difficulty
of being simply is not enough. There is
a project for the cousins of the sun.

· DIARY OF FEARS ·

1. I'M AFRAID TO LEAVE THIS ROOM

The electricity
is rested up and ready
to come out of the ground. But I'm
not. No one who comes

to the door is used
to the way things are.
But you can't see them anyway
because the light is back

from exile and keeps going
in the wrong direction.
I would too.

2. I'M AFRAID TO LEAVE THIS CHAIR

People who are lost
should stay put. I might miss
something. Someone of tremendous
intellectual power

might come to this chair
and I'd be gone. I made
up my mind, no matter where
I go, I will come back

to this chair. So why leave?

3. I'M AFRAID OF SAYING THE WRONG THING

One immediate sign
is loss of limb control.

You spill your coffee all down the hall.
Then the mind starts burning.

This is how you know
you've said a magic word.
You can take it back — you can say it again —
and still not turn evil

but you will lose most people.

4. I'M AFRAID OF EATING THE WRONG THING

Food calls out from the kitchen,
"Hey, pal, you're the most."
It gathers round expectantly
on the countertops.

So this is hunger, is it?
Flatterers, beware!
I'll chew your skin and crunch your bones
until you are no more

and then I'll lick the floor.

5. I'M AFRAID OF BEING OVERPOWERED

You're walking down the street
or sitting in your house
and bam! you're in a big brown sack
being carried off.

Your captor might be good.
He might be beautiful.
He might not — but you see no reason
not to twist your will

if twisting it will please him.

· POEM IN WHICH THE WORD TIME IS REPLACED BY THE WORD MISSILE ·

Missile. To sit down and write. I don't have missile & I want to write. Last night coming home. The driving. Like last night I wanted to come home TO something—like a fire in the fireplace, dogs. But like I don't have missile to do half the things. Coming home last night I wanted missile to think, missile to settle in & have someone—not a necessity; people are a constant aggravation. Well the missile I had was not mine; I sell missile & here is this machine. I hate my typewriter because every day I spend my missile working at it. Now I am trying to fill a spare room. Can't remember where the spare room is. There really was one a whole other wing. Like now I'm trying to find the room, decorate it. The kid can move in, a place all to himself. That's the other issue besides missile. Memory space. Empty. This is the missile for filling. I hate the way the missile all gets eaten up; we know we're going to die but we spend our missile like tomorrow. Tomorrow. And the reason is so nobody will find us unfit, nobody will put us in lockup, serving missile. Like if they find us unfit, incapable of making our own way, buying our own sofa, then they will say admonishingly—tall & admonishing: You don't know how to take care of yourself so you should be put away

you got to spend your waking hours constructively, not like a passiveaggressive planting boobytraps in the establishment; you got to be productive & keep going. Like, you get up early

& work on the typewriter. They all need you it's so nice. They give you money and if only, if only the Feds don't take your money then you can keep typing, you can get a better typewriter. And the things you postpone. Mostly going to sleep with a book on your chest, you don't have missile for frivolous novels or extramarital flirtations. Nothing serious. Then there's george who is gone all the missile

I started all this with the idea of making myself missile, making the shape of my own missile, holding my missile and being the boss and saying, now I can do this. Running out, all the missile, we know this we know it always do, about how one night you lie awake & go I don't want to go to sleep because it shuts off, my friend shuts off the thing in there that keeps me company; and someday it'll be gone completely, and I don't want to be so dead without that friend in there. Like if it could go on, just the friend inside the head to hell with the rest of it, no leaping flames, no moaning, no boredom really because you are just quietly with the friend inside and all the rest who cares

I work fast on this machine you know and so if I have an hour project, plan an hour. Have an hour tonight what to do. No more work tonight honey, don't do it. Stuffed w M&Ms fed some to the dogs they look sickly. Bang: if I had drums now then I could beat but clicking that's what it's about, clicking. Pretend this is bach. Music for the organism. See if you could see the lights going by something unclean, something far away from like making a shell which is what it is really about, nachre. You chew up things in the ocean & ooze them out & over missile they turn to whitish crust & you are okay for a lifemissile there inside but we keep pretending, tomorrow, in a year or two it will take missile the way the clash breath harvest beat take missile, the way the beat on the body inside; comes a missile of fever when nothing really is wrong if someone could just tell you, someone smile & say "Janet nothing is wrong this missile" mile of sand along the beach & a brandnew 5star hotel: this is what they want me to accept

nothing around but white beach overdone blank seabottom raised up out of the sea & nothing growing   it is a desert, really, a strip of desert w a 5star on the south china sea   & what about the plumbing, shall we eat nouvelle cuisine out here in the middle of nowhere, and where do the filipinos live, the busboys, the deskclerks, the bellhops where do they all live because there is not a village around until you get to the jungle where the revolution in little explosions happens. In Mindanao. So missile

there it would weigh on me white & heavy. All the bored ladies all the misfits. Unsuited I try to tell them to have fun, don't really like a good missile, I was kidnapped by fairies as a child & taught to take responsibility for the cobwebs in heaven   you know and I will never get to them but meanmissile I can type

missile you know imagine it taking off w a

flaming tail out of the ground near your farm. Imagine the trajectory of missile. Few short moments & everything you know changes, no more pig with the wooden leg. You know that joke. Crawl into your hole & like if anybody comes & says come on out, you know they're nuts & just after your canned goods. Hurts me to get so fat, waste my missile eating m&ms. missile missile missile

how you want it to hold you your own missile wrap you up make no missile for anything but this quiet friendship inside the head where we know what to do to keep the others from noticing us, we know how to keep them off   just let your missile eat you quietly & then you are free to think the things, like I love you inside your head, like there is an intrusion of sound something irresistible

a rosebud opening outside the window god knows the aphids have bored a hole through it. In the howling, in the night storm. but still a drama of thin red & roundness & uncontrolled lust. interior space losing it, getting lost in the air over missile. hold me you in there. with the brass knuckles in there you in the open marketplace. no developments, no missile, because in here we put a can around the interior & we go, you are mistaken. No one cares, everyone hurtles around taking a chance they'll kill you

hurtling around   missile goes by it kind of floats and your face changes but you can get it back,

the numbers add up and missile floats on by with
some nice music, you want to grab it and make it
your own forever, you got to hold it and squeeze
it with your best muscle   you got to fight your
missile & keep it from floating away to some
strange place   you got to be a hero, sit down and
ride

so much to get done, your stuff first I got to do
your stuff first and then when I get to this, this is
the last little minute I have! everybody thinks
tomorrow will be just the same as ever but I
know, I know. This is the endmissile. Maybe
nobody will give a shit about books. After the
end of missile who gives a shit about a balanced
phrase or two. On the beach clutching a battered
concordance to Milton. Where is night

foul mother of annoyance sad. So i had a project:
got up this morning & worked early, had to meet
a deadline. George is off somewhere making a
movie this missile is the best. We got to adjust to
this state of affairs him going off to work on
movies all the missile, and me well I have been
doing this a long missile, meet the customers
deadlines get the money and how it glides by the
missile. Can my goods, take them out some
missile later when we all need them the most. In
the evening I sit down at my machine & I hate it
because I have spent all my missile working for
other people   making money because I don't
want to give anybody a chance to say I am unfit
and spend my missile poorly

they will just say tsk tsk we were right all along,
women who open howling in the storm are

ruined   they will put me someplace for ruined women

I don't want to close my eyes at night   foul mother   who cares about all the rest   next week next year when I have the missile I will close my eyes and give the friend inside all my missile

then there's george   off someplace all the missile   I wanted to come home to something last night but no, not this missile   and who can expect it anyway they have their lives; and all I want really is for my missile to wrap me up   hold me   safe in this place where they don't know

what if one day your missile takes off like a rocket   climbs up out of the ground around your farm   glides up over your farm to some irresistible music   then you will know they're wrong when they say come out now you can come out   they just want your canned goods

The best persuaded of himself, so cramm'd (as he thinks) with excellencies that it is his grounds of faith that all that look on him love him; and on that vice in him will my revenge find noteable cause to work. (Shakespeare, *Twelfth Night*)

Boys don't have babies.

The surface on which you work (preferably marble), the tools, the ingredients and your fingers should be chilled throughout the operation . . . (Rombauer and Becker, *The Joy of Cooking*)

. . . we play with Molly, because Molly is a very anxious dog, and she's very funny. She has a very long neck, so I'll be—she'll go like this, and her ears will flop down, and I'll go like this: I'll sneak up and be behind her, and I'll go—here's her back and here's her head, and I'll go like this right where her legs are, and I'll stop her and I'll pull her back, and then I'll pick her up sometimes. I'll lie on the floor and I'll pick her up. Her legs—she'll be like this, and she'll be like this up in the air, and she'll be squirming and squirming. And so we'll go—we used to throw her in our pool, and she was starting to get sick because of it, so we stopped. But most dogs love to jump in the pool. You never get her out. So what we did—I'd say, "Wonder Molly!" and I'd go, "Bip-ba-bip-Bip-bip-beep," you know, charge her, and she's flinging me over, and it's impossible to catch her, because she goes behind chairs, and then you go on one side—it's a huge chair—you go on one side, and you go—and you get her and her head will be like this, and it's almost like, in this room about this big, she's about this big, she'll squirm around, turn around, and you know you'll be—I'd just sit there, I'd be charging her, 'cause she'd go, there's a table here, and a chair here, and there's a couch here, so she'd be—go right there, the steps are up here and there's a bump, you know. And they go like this, and they go—and I'd be here, and I'd go like this, and there's the wall right here, and the steps go up, and it'd be a short wall, say. I usually climb over and jump on the chair. So I'd be going like this, and the wall's here, and Molly's here, and I go BAM! And she goes under the chair, and I go right through the wall, and I go—

In the long run, we are all dead.

· *UNSPEAKABLES* ·

1.

There is a party in the elevator.
And only one door to the elevator shaft.
The floor does not reach the elevator floor.
The elevator man is handsome, a musician,
was once a handsome young musician.

2.

A Fritos truck passes between rows of trees.
It's pleasant, how it rocks, and silent.
This is the way evil works.

3.

"I keep a flame burning very low to the side,"
you say, and I excuse myself, go to the
    balcony,
and dry-heave until I slump by the door.

4.

If the wall were butter,
it would melt.
The wall lamps would sink.
"Mother and Son Kissing" would sink.
The wastebasket would be ruined.
The horsemen would show over the wall.

5.

A question not asked about absence of
    feeling

or what seems to be absence of feeling.
Lovers meet, the night is warm, there is
     fine rain,
light comes from several small sources,
they have eaten well in separate halls,
plans for the next move are complete.
Someone sings, "All night by the rose, rose,
all night by the rose I lay.
Durst I not the rose to steal
and yet I bore the fleur away."

· *NEW DIRECTIONS IN LITERATURE* ·

1. DRAPED ERECTIONS

I do not keep my erectile tissue outside
dangling around where surely it is not safe.
Instead I keep it in the vestibule.
As you gently spread the inner drapes
you see the delicate area they protect.
Here is where you pace
babbling about operatic passion.
The inner drapes connect to form a hood.
Underneath is my erectile tissue
plus lining the inner walls of the grand entrance.
In the old days this stuff was removed
for the convenience of the visitor —
you friction, you irritation, now
you are fascinated when the shaft
sticks out of its hood and the doorway
tightens while every bone and ligament
in me tunes its strings, exaggerates its faces,
doublechecks its props, sets up its elegant
    backdrops,
oils its tremendous gears, then starts the
    big production
and you squeeze in
pitying and terrified but safe.

2 . NUDE ERECTIONS

I wear the erectile tissue on my chest
out in cold air. This is not
an invitation but an involuntary
double aim, the work of warm blood
whose job is my comfort and survival —
I offer nothing. I get
more crazy than I mostly want to be. You
who come for my erectile tissue
get what your mouth expects.

Forget moms, forget big babies —
both of us are wounded to abstraction
and when I am mad, already
left this improbable breeding ground
for a theater that doesn't exist
I give you my erectile tissue, let
your sucking shrink my empty mind
and have ink, give ink.